My Keys to
Allah's Love

First published in the UK by Bright Books,
an imprint of Beacon Books and Media Ltd
Earl Business Centre, Dowry Street, Oldham, OL8 2PF, UK.

First edition published in 2022

www.beaconbooks.net

ISBN 978-1-915025-44-9 PB
ISBN 978-1-915025-45-6 HB
ISBN 978-1-915025-46-3 EB

Cataloging-in-Publication record for this book is available from the British Library

The text was checked and approved by Sharia expert Shaikh Bilal Brown,
CEO & Founder at Marifah Institute
www.marifahinstitute.com

www.dariavolyanskaya.com

My Keys to
Allah's Love
Understanding My Religion

Written and Illustrated by
Daria Volyanskaya

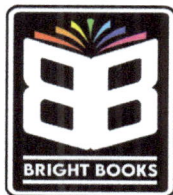

BRIGHT BOOKS

بسم الله الرحمن الرحيم

١٤٣٠

IN THE NAME OF ALLAH,
THE MOST GRACIOUS, THE MOST MERCIFUL

Kids, who cares about you the most in the world? Mum and dad, right?

That's absolutely right but someone cares for you more than your parents do. Allah cares for you more than anyone in the world. He has given you a beautiful life, a loving mother and a superman daddy. He made you a smart little Muslim!

But how can we make Allah love us even more and become His favourites?

The fun part of this is that you don't need to give anything away! You only need to do what He loves and avoid what He dislikes.

Aisha and Noor are also interested in getting to know Allah, our Creator. So, let's discover together what the keys to Allah's love are!

Allah is
Our Only God

We as little Muslims, believe that there is no god but Allah and Muhammad ﷺ is His Messenger.

Allah created us and the universe around us all by Himself. He has no son, no daughter, no wife, no mother, no father and no one created Him. Wow! Can you imagine His power? He did everything by Himself. Although we cannot see Him, He sees us. Every time we think of Him, He thinks of us too. So when we are happy, sad, scared or angry, we should remember Allah. He is always there for us when we need help. When we wish for something, we should only ask Him. Who can help us better than the owner of the whole universe? Everything good in our life comes from Him, and everything bad, He can help us to fix! So our first key to Allah's love is to believe that He is our only God.

Imagine yourself riding a bicycle. If you grabbed one handle of the bicycle, and your friend grabbed the other, and both of you steered it together, would you be able to keep the balance? It would fall and crash. If Allah had a partner, companion, or any equal in power and might, the world would be in disorder.

Quran 3:18

4

Salah

Have you ever wished to talk to the King of the entire universe, Allah?

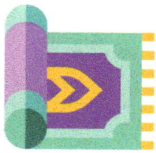

It must be so exciting! It is possible and the way you can do it is through Salah. Salah means prayer. Whenever we offer a prayer, we talk to Allah and He replies to us too. Salah is like a private phone call between you and Allah and the Adhan (call for prayer), is like an invitation from Allah to every Muslim to talk to Him. If we pray on time, Salah will protect us from bad thoughts and actions.

Did you know that angels also perform Salah? Every creation in the world worships Allah, but we are special because we can talk to Allah through prayer.

When we miss a prayer, Allah becomes unhappy with us. So, let's never miss a meeting with our Kind Creator, Allah!

Quran 2:238

Allah is our only God
And He created all the world,
The moon, the sun, the day, the night
And the Quran to be our guide.

He sent His prophets to the earth
To teach us wise and fair rules:
To do good deeds, to pray and fast.
This way of life is called Islam!

How can a Muslim talk to God?
That's right, they can perform Salah!
To clean their mind and their soul
And make their bad thoughts very small!

Five times a day we ask Allah
To guide us on our path of life,
And sure, He will be with us,
Until we pray with all our hearts!

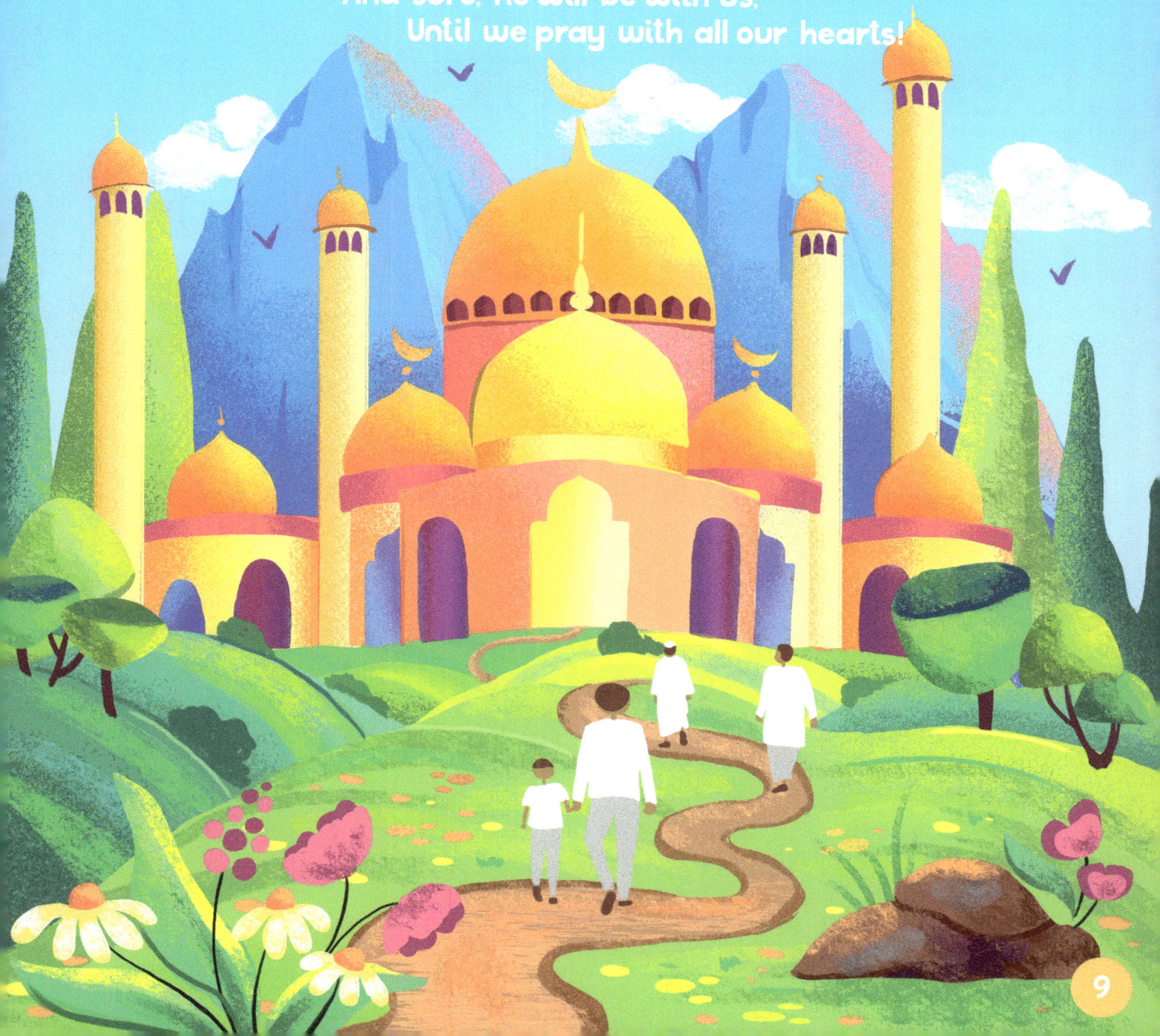

Zakah

Allah cares about poor people, that's why He asked us to pay Zakah. It is a small part of our money that we give away every year. This is a secret key to make our hearts and wealth pure.

When we give Zakah, we help poor children who don't have enough clothes, or children who don't have any toys, or have nothing to eat at lunchtime because their parents don't have enough money for food.

But how much money do we have to give away? Won't it be hard? Oh no, not at all! Allah made it so easy for us.

Let's imagine that you have ten slices of cucumber. Cut the last slice into four pieces and give just one of them to the poor.

With just that little piece, we can change the lives of many people and gain the love of Allah.

Quran 2:110

Fasting in
Ramadan

Ramadan is the month in which we show Allah that we love Him by fasting from sunrise to sunset. Fasting means we can't eat, drink or behave badly. But why would Allah want us not to eat or drink?

Firstly, Allah wants you to understand how hard it is for poor people to feel hungry and thirsty all the time. He wants you to feel mercy and share with them the good things you have. Allah also wants to reward us so He gives us a chance to share. That's why in Ramadan we always feed the poor. That's why we thank Allah for the tasty food we have every day.

Secondly, Allah wants you to fight your bad habits. He wants you to get used to showing only good behaviour and manners. Can you imagine the best servant of Allah cheating, lying, or screaming angrily? Would Allah like such behaviour? Of course not! So let's show our best character because Allah will be happy with us.

Quran 2:183

Every good Muslim pays Zakah
From money given by Allah.
We give this money to the poor
Who don't have clothes, a home, or food.

It's a small part of what we have
From money that we earned this year.
It's tiny but it helps a lot
To get a great reward from God!

13

Muslims are brothers in Islam
Who help the poor in Ramadan.
Who share goods and also feed
Everyone hungry and in need.

We cannot eat or drink but patience
Will help us fight our bad habits.
We read a lot and follow the Quran
To get rewards in Ramadan!

Hajj

Allah calls all His beloved people to His house every year, and this is called Hajj. Hajj means to go on a pilgrimage. This means at least once in their life every adult Muslim should travel to the holy city of Makkah in Saudi Arabia, and visit the Kaaba, the House of Allah. Just imagine visiting Allah's most beloved mosque on the Earth. Sounds amazing, right?

The Kaaba was built by Allah's beloved Prophet Ibrahim. Muslims from every corner of the world come to Hajj. They wear special white clothes and become equal in front of the Merciful Allah. They ask Him to erase all their bad actions and forgive them for everything wrong. Hajj is one of the keys to clean our hearts and gain Allah's forgiveness for any mistakes we have made.

Quran 22:27

Equality

Allah created us all so beautiful and different – some are short, others are tall, some are brown like chocolate, others are white like ice-cream!

Allah created us to be different because He wanted us to learn to be fair with everyone.
If your friend is chubby and you are thin, it doesn't mean that you are better. If you have only a few toys and your friend has a whole pile of toys, it doesn't mean that Allah loves him or her more. No!

What is important to Allah is your heart. He loves those who have honest and kind hearts. And He doesn't like anyone to think that they are better than others. We are only better to Allah if we have a good character! We will earn His love if we treat each other equally and fairly.

Quran 7:13

Allah invites us to make Hajj
To visit His amazing house.
This journey should be done one time
In every single Muslim's life.

We'll wear special shiny clothes,
All pure white and tidy robes,
We'll ask and hope Allah forgives
All our mistakes and our bad deeds.

Allah won't like us hurting others
Because He made all Muslims brothers.
We should have mercy and protect
Each other's right to have respect.

So I won't laugh and call bad names,
I'd better give some compliments!
I'll never make fun of somebody,
I'd better make him my best buddy!

Remembering
Allah

Let me tell you another secret key to gaining Allah's love. This key is to remember Him and talk to Him. Are you wondering how you can talk to Allah? That's so simple. Just say **bismillah** before you start doing anything and Allah will support you. Say a **dua** before you go to bed or wake up and He will protect you. Allah likes being called for help and He likes when we pray to Him.

BISMILLAH

The word 'bismillah' simply means 'In the name of Allah'. Any important work that does not begin with bismillah is imperfect. Let's say 'bismillah':

• Before we eat or drink.
• When we enter or leave the house.
• When we start any good deed or useful task.
• When we feel pain.

When your alarm clock is buzzing in the morning, you always turn to it immediately. Something similar happens when you keep remembering Allah. Your dua is like an urgent call too! He listens to you immediately, and He will also mention you to His angels. Allah loves when we ask Him.

Quran 17:110

Thinking deeply about the
Creation

Have you ever wondered how a cloud can hang in the sky with no support?
Who gives food to the big whales in the sea?
How does the sun rise from the east and set in the west?

Everything in the universe is designed by Allah. He orders the clouds to stay in the sky, the sun to rise and gives food to all creatures. Look how your body is growing on its own and how the sea is home to a million types of fishes. How amazing!

Allah wants us to think about the beauty of His creation. Every big and little thing that Allah created is very special and important, including you! He made you so beautiful and smart.

Every creature, even the furious tiger and the quirky monkey, was given a purpose: to worship Allah alone.

Allah wants us to notice the beauty of His creation and think about His mercy.

Quran 3:191

Allah loves when I talk to Him,
He likes to hear all my prayers
And I can ask for anything
That makes me or my actions better!

Bismillah!

Bismillah!

When we start
any task

When we enter
home

Bismillah!

Before we eat
or drink

I start my day with bismillah.
I say it with my every action!
Before bedtime I read duas,
And wake up with Allah's protection.

Allah is controlling everything,
Our every breath, our every blink.
He makes the clouds pour with rain.
He makes the night turn into day.

He made all creatures so amazing,
All nature vibrant and breathtaking!
He gave a purpose to us all,
To worship Him and Him alone.

Allah knows
Everything

Allah is watching everything and even a leaf from a tree can't hide from Him. He sees you when no one else does. He ordered angels to follow you and write everything you do in a diary. The angel on your right writes all your good deeds, and the angel on your left writes all your bad deeds. Not a single moment can slip away from them. So let's be careful and try to do only good deeds!

Allah wrote everything that will happen in His Universe in a special book a very long time ago, way before He created us. Allah wrote some happy moments for everyone, but also some tests and trials. Allah wants to discover which of us will thank Him at a happy time and be patient in a hard moment. He wants to see who is going to do good deeds and help fellow Muslims. Allah wants to reward us for the best of our deeds!

Quran 22:70

Rewards of Allah

Everyone loves gifts! And Allah likes to reward His beloved people for their good deeds. The key to His love is to work for His amazing rewards:

• Allah gives special protection to believers who obey Him. He sends angels to protect children from the evil eye and bad people. How cool is it to have your own bodyguards!

• Allah makes His beloved servants stronger and helps them to do even more good deeds. He puts light in their hearts to help them see the wrong and the right. He saves them from anger and laziness.

• Allah removes sadness from their hearts when they remember Him. He gives them patience, peace and strength when they are in trouble. He rewards them with a brilliant mind to learn new things and memorise the Quran.

• Allah's biggest reward is Jannah! There we will be so close to Allah and His prophets. Paradise will be filled with your favourite toys, sweets and foods. You won't ever get sick or sad there, and you can do everything you wish.

Quran 24:38

29

Allah is watching all of us,
He knows our future and our past
And He sent angels to record
Our every deed and every word.

So I will try to make my book
Full of good deeds and kind words.
This is a great thing that I know
Will make Allah love me a lot!

Allah has many gifts for me,
He has rewards for each good deed!
Those who remember Him a lot
Will get His help and His support.

HAPPINESS

PEACE

PROTECTION

And if I make my best effort
To be a good Muslim in this world,
Allah will build for me a house
In His majestic paradise.

WRONG

RIGHT

HELP &
SUPPORT

GUIDANCE

www.ingramcontent.com/pod-product-compliance
Lightning Source LLC
Chambersburg PA
CBHW041636040426
42448CB00023B/3495